SPLITTING OFF

TRINY FINLAY

NIGHTWOOD EDITIONS
ROBERTS CREEK, BC
2004

SPLITTING OFF

Nightwood Editions
R.R. #22, 3692 Beach Ave.
Roberts Creek, BC
Canada VON 2W2

Edited for the house by Silas White
Typesetting by Carleton Wilson

We gratefully acknowledge the support of the Canada Council for the Arts and the British Columbia Arts Council for our publishing program.

NATIONAL LIBRARY OF CANADA CATALOGUING IN PUBLICATION

Finlay, Triny, 1976–
    Splitting off / Triny Finlay.

Poems.
ISBN 0-88971-198-4

    I. Title.

PS8611.I65S65 2004   C811'.6   C2004-900701-7

*For Catherine Chapman, at one end,
and for Drew Kennickell, at the other.*

CONTENTS

I: LIKING CHOCOLATE AGAIN

Feed from my tongue
Touch my wet hip
Give me words
Give me words

   —Lisa Robertson, *Debbie: An Epic*

PINK PILLS

You know me best at breakfast, before the eggs have cracked, before the cream has soured in its pewter jug. I fell out of love for my own good, took small pink pills to prevent more scars. I don't eat chicken or red meat and I just started liking chocolate again. And scallops. And shrimp. I drink a lot of tea, labour at the *New York Times* crossword puzzles. I have no moles, but I'm punctuated by. Random. Freckles. Sometimes they're raised, or arranged in celestial patterns. I judge people by their eyes, and by how much they need me. I am trying not to expect so much perfection. Heart disease and diabetes run in my family, I'm having an ultrasound Friday, I'm usually in a hurry but I'm slowing down. I grew up thinking herpes lurked on every toilet seat. Last year I read that cold sores, chicken pox, and shingles all stem from the same virus. I have had each and they do not seem so similar. I like hospitals, and outrageous memories, but I wanted you to know how much I like vanilla ice cream (food will always lead me somewhere).

Bottle it, not like nail enamel or department store perfume, but like sauce for your next meal, better than satay. You know you love it with jasmine rice, you know it goes well with wine. It was a sweater you wore in junior high, flecked, so itchy you needed a cotton turtleneck between it and your pubescent surfaces. It was a scuffed pair of penny loafers, deep-pocket sugar sack pants, a skinny leather tie you wore on an Eastern airlines flight to Fort Lauderdale. In your bedroom it was rosebuds on the filmy curtains, Holly Hobby's silhouette, plates behind the dresser-drawer pulls. Icing on the cake, rubber arm bands, a note for a boy in Abaco. Gymsuits. Every eraser. Too much while it lasted. When you shaved your head it all went out with the garbage, like the baby, the bath water. What covered you and your sensitive skin like gravy, thick and starched, disappeared like a plucked eyebrow, gone for a time, back to challenge your dismissal.

...the baby is sleeping, the green has begun to emerge from the rind of the cantaloupe, and everything seems possible.

−Robert Hass, "Museum"

A holiday, doesn't matter where to. Set a plastic-bauble bottle of Pepsi in the drink holder and drive east. Think of the shiny black telephone like an injured stag beetle in her den while she's speaking with her mother. Read all signage. Choose the first exit with the word 'blueberry' in it, maybe Oxford, because there's a fresh pie roosting on the gummy back seat. Sleep with her friend's friend in a single-person tent while you're waiting for the next car ferry. Don't sleep. Don't try to please anyone. Answer three unasked questions aloud: *mauve asters; the Book of Ruth; pink cotton underwear.* Memorize the dream you had last night. Her mother's house: a sandal floating through the open kitchen window, everyone hungry for barley, winnowing themselves, famine like a feminine itch. Wait for her to bite into the last slice of melon before unhooking the bra. Stop the car when you want to get out.

Coming down from the first buss high, I withdraw, flashes of your sweet, gapped-teeth lacunae infuriating the room. We were side by side on a GO train, tense at the thought of salt-licked skin and the ticket-taker's schedule. We got off before our stop, certain we'd be discovered. At the old Eaton's downtown we sat atop a book display, reading novels as flip-books, fanning the pages with swift-riff thumbs. Strands of black words swirled together like wet tea leaves, shaping themselves into stick-figured dancing girls, oak limbs we'd scaled. I took your pulse because it seemed so obscure, soft rhythms that had been there all along, sheltered in the city's filth. After the nurse act we snickered; I described a plastic produce bag, clear, full of tampons like rusted car parts. You thought I was making it up, filling your head with distractions so that we could kiss again. But there it was, in the lane beside you, so low it hadn't caught your eye.

She takes me to Lolita's Lust for cocktails and kalamari. I order a Shirley Temple. She flinches, inflates her pinched jowls, steers the conversation toward golf. Talking about the pace, the swing, the quest for the lowest score. I stab an orange slice with the point of my tiny umbrella, disturbing its balancing act on the glass rim. Excuse myself. In the ladies' room I take off my pantyhose, push it into the calm bowels of my purse. Back at the table, I lower myself into the club chair, lifting my silk skirt to let the leather breathe against my bared skin. She says, *There's the lovely lady*, stirs her Sling with a steak knife. Titters with her tongue between her teeth. I sit in the warm flesh seat thinking I'd like to work my pinking shears along her edges, finish her off like a French seam.

PINK SNEAKERS

In a tin-roofed town the sidewalks bisect poop-strewn lawns. Watch your step. Mail carriers have known this for years, wear rubber soles, follow mathematical routes. Don't always deliver. If you wear pink sneakers in this town, be warned: kids on skateboards will smile, bank tellers will swoop like benevolent night herons. Walk quickly when you walk at all, avoid standing in lines, choose indoor dining over open patios. If the sneakers are new, and made of suede or canvas, never wear them in the rain. The dye will bleed like beets into your feet, leaving you stained in cotton-candy splendour. If the sneakers are old, wear them everywhere. People you pass will believe in things they hadn't before thought possible, convinced by the value of snug, jarring footwear. But don't fool yourself into thinking it proceeds from here. Eschew pink jeans, pink tank tops, pink cashmere sweaters. The force is sudden, and limited to shoes.

II: THE WORLD WE ALREADY KNEW

they propose that we are a bridge holding hands above water. they discuss the implications of letting go

    –Nicole Markotić, "platypus love v"

ORANGE PLASTIC CHAIR

This is the hour to move:
tipping over the telephone
table before you hang

up, dragging the uncoiled
cord across linoleum.
Press your back flat against

the cinder-block wall, flat
as it will go, slide down
as if there were an orange

plastic chair supporting
your thighs, your newly knobby
knees. Stay this way until

the visitors arrive,
until the loneliest
nurse has filled a frosted

blue vase with slow-dripping
water. Then move away,
sop up the puddle

she left at the sink with
the stiff hem of your gown
and wring it out quickly.

DREAMING YOUR ANAPHYLAXIS

In a parkette, on Bathurst, a bench
I passed by chance. You and the swelling,
foreign protein, one more reaction.

How many times have I asked
how to work the EpiPen,
which end to open, which to stab you with.

The chest will not quite fall.

Something this obvious—
respiratory distress, the city,
a black x marked on the skin—
bears repeating,

waits behind the eyes like a bruised hip
under corduroy jeans.

Evidence of something real,
sensitivity,
panic and the bleak collapse of circulation,
inappropriate, waiting.

PREPARATIONS FOR BEAUTIFYING WOMEN

If Esther had a camera, to snap
a life record, she might tease
the spurious queen with images
of soft-shelled girls mooning,

oiling their maidenhead, myrrh
and lust in equal portions. She
might bring you a stippled portrait
of Mordecai at the gates, worrying

his own knuckled hide as he waits,
like you, for the next big thing.
She might find you, beg for fresh
aloe while you work at the kitchen

table, creaming sugar with butter
and a double shot of vanilla. She might
slip past you, run tap water
behind a locked bathroom door

until you're sure there will be blood
on the floor tiles. She might sing
show tunes. Let her hold you,
let her pull grey hairs from your

scalp. Let her camera woo you.
Pose at the balcony rail
with the last icicle of winter,
drawing her in, changing the subject.

VIRGIN'S BATHROOM

Your poor crate filled with those
tiny Christmas clementines now
the only fruit in your apartment.
I peel them, make pachyderm
portraits for your collection.
They harden, hanging one tack
each on your wall.

I've been meaning to swim,
to choose water this time
over asphalt and dried cranberries,
things I covet along with rehydration.
Would change it all for tomorrow
soaking nightmares in your bath,
colloidal oatmeal oil clinging
to the golden down along my winter skin.

The men are sober and deliberate, inching their way through my dreams. Some are dressed in brown, creeping up the basement steps behind me, turning a corner, toward me, after school. Like taxicabs, they idle nearby. When I was six I danced ballet in a United Church parlour with other small white girls. We were always early for class, hungry, waiting together in the Sunday school room. One winter afternoon I step into the hall before the others, all seamed tights and feet pushed into skinny pink slippers. My eyes catch on a tall figure in the stairwell to my right. A man. Younger than our dads. Like the man we find in the city glen, my sisters and me. His fly unzipped, rubbing his penis against the bark of a broad oak tree. This might be my earliest memory. He follows us up the steep ravine, hopeless, incoherent. One sister clears a path to the world we already knew; one sister pulls me onto her back, wears me like an anorak, whispers, *Don't look behind you.*

DOG AT THE NORTH SIDE

Rankled, snapping her carcassy name
(Cass! Cass! Cass-iiii-dy!)
I listen for clinking tags
—this city, that city, microchip,
rabies—wait, like a child

in late-June moonlight, for the game
to be finished, for Mum to call,
The streetlights are on, once
the others have gone in behind
Peggy's shed to murder one another

in the dark. At the pebbly beach
on the north side of the river
my pale dog has broken through
thick bramble to devour
an evening appetizer.

The game isn't finished, fish
are rotting on this shore and the spoils
leak slowly through the air.
Mosquitoes punish me for playing,
for flattening the thicket in one

sure path toward water.
She sees me, eats well: bones
filling her salty mouth, crushed
between scrubbed teeth.
I pull her ruff, click

leash into collar and steer
us, scraped, sticky,
back across the old
train bridge. We hold
the pong in our pores.

As we walk, I slacken the lead,
watch murky stains along her slim
legs pace us. I plan the next
meal—shrimp, cream, sundried
tomatoes—before we reach

the ravaged willow straining
against our fence posts; the young
cat wailing into our screen door;
a filled water dish waiting for a fetid
tongue to stroke its steely rim.

FANCY DRESS

I

Onstage, it was something. And off. Before
I knew you, this was the one thing I clung

to, packed with every move. It hung
in the bedroom closet like a skinned

cushion, velvet in the deepest shade
of blood. I must have pilfered it from

the costume loft, once the show
was finished and routine life resumed; I must

have eased it onto a thin wire hanger
and crushed it between notebooks in my bag,

a memory of pin-curls and zinging lips fooling
me into circles of vodka martinis and consecrated

couture. But I never wore it with you;
it was too long, too flagrant, too awkward,

the zipper protruding at the back and the hem
crudely basted if you considered it closely.

II

The first trip to your home is light and nothing
like a ritual. Deplaning, alone, I am struck

by the surreal Bermuda sun. In my taut
black suit and heels, I swish and click, pale,

compressed, toward the terminal. The breeze
smothers, the Customs agent probes

my baggage, clears my name. I find you, once
my eyes have adjusted to the light, a barefoot

and subtly stubbled fiancé-in-waiting. Don't
say that I'd expected something else—pomp,

a swarm of anxious relatives, witness
to this union. You fold me into the back

seat of the sun-spoiled car. I lean,
the left hand flung through the window,

the right one holding on, fitted for the old
road's tight, cambered, low-walled ride.

III

We bought one, periwinkle blue, short,
for my middle sister, the luckless maid

of honour. Ten months early we planned
the routine details, long-distance,

white slipcovers for the vinyl chairs
and free drinks until 1 AM. My mother

sampled cake in remote bakeries,
relating each mouthful of battered

bliss over the phone. *We should have let
the machine get it*, you said, every time

she called, setting the receiver in my hand
as if it were a colicky infant. Like they say,

I let it all roll off me, the swing band,
the buffet, the invitation font. It was enough

to have donned a ring on that weakest
of fingers, the diamond sunken and gleaming.

IV

For me, we took my other sister's creamy
raw silk gown to the old Greek seamstress,

who snipped the offending shoulder
straps, boned the bodice. In the fitting

room the beaded seed pearls chafed
my biceps, flickered in the artificial

light. The old woman's hands pressed
my scant cleavage down beneath

the crisp fabric. She eyed my tattooed ankle,
straight pins clamped between dry, dour lips.

I asked for a tiara and elbow-length
gloves, pranced through the narrow shop

in my own slimmed version of classical balance.
Everyone beamed. My breasts felt trapped

like fine fresh linen waiting to shift
and slip out of the napkin ring.

V

One detail we never did resolve, though
the thing loomed, tense and stringy, suspended

like a rope bridge over a gorge. Our friends
chided me, said you might show up

in your beaten steel-toed boots, sandstone
dust and metal filings stuck to your beard.

I left it with you, the florist's refrain:
And what will the groom be wearing?

As if a simple fashion matter might
tell all. Later, we arrive separately

at someone else's wedding. We've made
it through whiteouts, unanswered

mail, and we are here to paint the town, red
as Eylie's Bhutanese gown. This time

my dress is new, steamed smooth, seams pressed
flat against my skin. Moving with my body. Fitting.

AFTERWARDS

She drives to that section of town she usually avoids: lavish jewellers, strained and bowing booksellers, bakeries with their fancy display cakes, boutiques with their genuine white silk dresses. All the way to the dark pub on the north side of the street, the place where she will sit on a low stool and sip a pint of raspberry wheat beer. And another. And when the woman beside her motions for her to move closer, to share the newspaper she's been reading, she does. Without saying a word, without learning the other woman's name, she spends an afternoon absorbing birth and death announcements, swallowing imported beer and pine nuts, realizing that what she needs now, what she believes she needs, is the sense of having been somewhere.

TEMPLE ON THE GORE ROAD

We don't have words
for this kind of incongruity,

ancient beauty replicated
on Canadian soil, plunked
at the edge of the subdivision,
postcard ziggurat.

We drive south into the city
on a Thanksgiving Monday
while the cars going north
queue along the Gore Road, idling
as if caught mid-parade. We are going
the wrong way for worship—

a lineup we will never join,
        not for the pantheonic rush,
        not for the budget homes,
        not for the wonder.

But we will stop for fresh corn at the side
of the road, for funeral processions, red lights.

We've chosen our temples, our gods,
and now their resplendence defies us.

III: SPLITTING OFF

. . . until the nail is hit, it doesn't believe in the hammer.

—Julia Alvarez, *In the Time of the Butterflies*

SELF-PORTRAIT AS THE GOODERHAM FLATIRON BUILDING

I

You can try to make me fit
into the lot you've made
ready. You won't need a crane
or the usual team of stalwart
men.

II

Look again. I am here because
    of the way the lake met the map, because
      of that conflict between the ego and the land, because
    the angle wasn't right.
Because Front Street follows the curve of the shore
and Wellington lines up with the others.

III

You think I am different.
You don't know difference.

Use me like the rest: the castle, the tower, the dome.
As landmark, as marker
for stunned intruders.
As object of worship.

Everyone wants their own slice
of the pie. I prefer the making.

SELF-PORTRAIT AS MY OWN BRAIN TUMOUR

This, love, is an imagined world.
Things go up and down, in and out
like grubs in the butterfly garden,
like death-ready shadflies, mouths sealed against the future.

Let's talk about the brain, how
it's been murkier than salt marsh water, how
it slips in its own cranial puddles,
will implode without warning.

       It's a snake in the grass.
       A black pearl.
       You can't see it but it knows you are watching.
       You can't see it but it hides anyway.

Let's talk about vision, the image you might
have if we'd been in the same dream:
       a sagging barn before it falls,
       a slab of Fundy ice before it shifts,
       a muskrat's tail before it slides into the reeds.

       Carve me. Pry me out.

What good is a kept secret, where does it go
when the pain ends?

SELF-PORTRAIT AS EKPHRASTIC TENSION

Let's call it what it is: desire,
or hope, or chaos. Something

sublime—a gilded frieze you touched
in Brussels, for love, in the public square;

a vase you carried on your back through
Asia because, though it cracked

along the way, you thought it was sacred.
What you should know about hope

is that it can't be pinned down. Either
you feel it or you don't and don't

mistake it for desperation. The old
stone will shift because of your

fingers; sugar peas snap.
The morning light in your living

room will catch every gap
in the vase if you glue it back together.

Forget Penelope and the putting off
of suitors. This is the thing you pass

every day, pass and forget, but

>   I know about that foetus on the sidewalk,
>   curled and pale pink like a half-cooked shrimp, out
>   of range.

>   So I left it there to bake—there will be more.

Tell me the secret about your dead boy and I'll show you
where I watched another bird baby drop,
the quick, feathered death, a second to match
the second.

Leave them and they will learn to fly eventually.

Come closer. Tell me the other secrets too.

>   Don't weave them into a story for your in-laws.
>   Don't pick them apart.
>   We are all killers, as weak as our words. Let us
>   push you from your desperate high-wire act.

SELF-PORTRAIT AS ONE MORE POTATO

This is not the kind you mash, or bake; don't waste
me, don't spread me around that way,

don't boil it all out of me. I don't boil
down to the thick and rich.

Don't leave me in a cool paper
bag below the sink. Never peel me.

I am an idea you had before you met me.
I can go for days without food.

You can't name me in the singular.
I am more than this. Dress me up,
dress me down. Trace my roots
and you can lay me anywhere.

Sit with me on a settee, or leave me alone.
Paint me as if I were   a woman
                           a package bound with twine
                           a wall for your graffiti—

Quote Ingres. Quote Christo. And Haring.

Yeah, I was Irish once. Then I split
off into something over here,
        something gold,
        something with too many eyes.

SELF-PORTRAIT AS SOMETHING YOU KEEP IN YOUR WALLET

I've been known to slip between the bills.
I am a list of vegetables you bought last winter.
I am a phone number in Fredericton.

You look for me.
You find me.
I move among your things like a green lynx spider.

What you might not understand
is that I lose everything
with longing—
     never the keys to the house,
     never the book of names,
but the important things—
     the taste of your tongue at the end
     of an afternoon of summer planting;
     the pulse that flicked between our hands
     when the car spun in the highway slush, turning
     away from the drop, turning away.

I am the code you were given
when you started the new job.
I am so long you have to write me down.

I am flat, compact, ready to wear. I tear easily.
You like my plain style.

> Take me with you to the ball.
> I can be transformed
> for an hour or two.
> We can slow-dance.

Remind yourself that there is beauty in more than just things.

SELF-PORTRAIT AS SONNET 54

A love poem you can understand.

A love poem has   a subject
                   an object
                   a reason for being around.

Copy it into your little brown book,
take it with you to Paris,
read it aloud in line at Notre Dame.

You can memorize it, dig it into the last dim ridge of your brain,
crack it open like a walnut,   let yourself be the he,
                               let yourself be the she.

A love poem you can smush into a business envelope,
squeeze into the paper cut on your ring finger—
        speak slowly, get close up, let the words sink in.

Spin it on your burnt tongue   on the subway
                                at the No Frills
                                in the privacy of your bathroom.

It was written before. It never grows old. It sings you to sleep.

It waits for you at the edge of the mirror.

SELF-PORTRAIT AS DAISY AND VIOLET HILTON

Two in one, two in the bush: where
does it end, you, and I?

Lick our ears with your suffragette
tongues; we are wondrous
and awful; single, single;

intimate, companionate.

We grow in the freak show forest.
We sing from the base of our spines.

We are the two-headed monster
in your terrorized landscape, waiting
for you, Scylla-like, by the whirlpool.

Let me be your compass, never
pointing North.

Would you separate me, put me under
(a spell   a knife   a blast of anaesthetic),
kill me?

I am solvent. Fluid.
Difficult to arrange.

But oh, when we play,
we sort ourselves inside out.

IV: CONFIDENCE TRICKS

You are moving like blood calmly within your own body.

—Michael Ondaatje, "Her House"

INCEPTIONS OF SKIN

You open me, as if biting into
the walnut-dusted skin of a small goat cheese
ball, as if lifting a piece of the skull puzzle
to catch a frame of my headspace reserved

for men riding bicycles: there you are.
I start, mark your patent lips as my ribs
sharpen against yours: the whetstones

of rapture. And when I face your spine, not
yet sleeping, tapping words in Morse code,
each vertebra resists one last brush
with vertigo before calibration.

THE SHAPE OF YOUR TONGUE

since feeling is first
who pays any attention
to the syntax of things
will never wholly kiss you

—e.e. cummings, "since feeling is first"

spread me across a slice
of the round flax loaf you baked
for your mother. use
a blunt knife. melt me
in an iron pot to fortify
me. salt me to arouse thirst.
fill me with sugared raspberries
to bleed in my pastry
if i bake or burst,
since feeling is first.

who pays any attention
to the shape of the tongue
as it forms my name in your
mouth? blend my blood
with heavy cream, measure
me with your hands, by the rings
of sprung curls at my neck. pull
the locks and let them go
knowing what this tension brings
to the syntax of things.

knead my creases with your lips.
hold me by both hips firmly
and roll me in your unbleached
flour skin—dust lifts
fingerprints from you.
slip me through each pore, stew
my bones until we fall
asleep without touching;
wait for the trace of tissue
(i will never wholly kiss you).

Sharing an upright shower for one
year. Peeling boiled beets.

Your rough wool, my needles,
knitting socks in September.

You plot me
co-ordinates,

the ache beneath callused skin,
bruised creases.

Your telephone voice: hold   the body
the wire   I will never be smooth

again. A dance—I've brought you to the
beach. You will not swim.

SACKVILLE, SEASON 2

We fight rancid winds all summer.
The doors won't seal us,

plain men sit in parked
pick-ups   looking.

I know the lies
already. Believe it.

The plates are clean. My
hands   slip

squeezing old avocados into bread
batter   and no garden to forget.

We sew quilts at night when
the flannel won't stifle,

you bake black olive
stuffing   bare.

Can't decide what binds the bones
together   the next easy life.

WHAT SHE DIDN'T SAY

Sometimes you smell like two old plums in a wire
hanging basket, unpitted.

You forget to listen for cellos, but I've seen
strings move you, fingers striding along a bass line.

November will bruise you; nights you will eat sourdough
bread with sliced brick cheese if only to bite into something.

Your eyes leave stains on my skin, broad blue
blots sinking through into my soft liver when you're gone.

To make tear ducts they cut into her, a surgical release while the bones in her ears thundered like luna moths. Now she buys fabric with insect patterns, slicing the fibrous bias in a single motion, dissecting. The quilts are pieced together, slowly, as unfinished as her own body. To make him fit they cut into her, knock her out and snip the thick rind she's been stretching for years. Pears decompose on the counter. She loses her taste for fresh fruit. The suture is looped and snarled like damp pubic hair, a reminder of bound edges, a knot, the blanket stitch. She will refuse future operations. She will sew each strip by hand, worry the cloth, poke it over and over with her one good needle while she tests for the proper tension.

NEW WOOL

I

The ex-lover returns to town
to sing for her supper,
voice swinging in a breezy
blue dress, strapless,
asking, *What's the biggest
secret you ever kept?*

She forgets the hardwood chill
we had that winter, the dog
on the duvet, breathing
at our toes.

II

You find it under the bed,
behind the dresser—the hair
of the dog that bit you.
Stow it. Pass it along
to the one who got away.
Or card it, spend endless nights
spinning new wool, a new look
for the next act.

III

I left her with a sandwich
bag, the dog's pale hairs
inside, locked with a polymer
zip. Enough to knit-purl-
knit socks for the kitchen.
And a note: *We may meet
next time with fur
in our pockets.*

TYPOLOGIES

I: *Tall and Quiet*

She takes me to the market, holds my hand
like a mother, lures me through the ranks
of fusty cheese. My thewless hips waver.
She takes me to the market, holds my hand
as if skin were our only connection, a quick
slip on the fish-gut floor and we're divided.
She takes me to the market, holds my hand
like a mother, lures me through the ranks.

II: *Maid in the Meadow*

Her omelettes seduce me, always
the freshest eggs, the thickest cream.
I could shock her lavish body anywhere.
Her omelettes seduce me, always
folded neatly, scallion scales spilling
out in vermicular trails. Her spices,
her omelettes, seduce me. Always
the freshest eggs, the thickest cream.

III: *Stout-Hearted*

If only her clothes pegs were fiercer. If only
we'd gauged the distance from here to town
I might have lingered like an aging damselfly.
If only her clothes pegs were fiercer. If only
she'd shown me the best way to test the wind
before allowing our rich, wrung skin to drip-dry.
If only her clothes pegs were fiercer, if only
we'd gauged the distance from here to town.

IV: *Demon Lover*

What could we do that you hadn't already
done? I only wanted a sly kiss, red wine;
but you needed bloodshed, shaved ice, gin.
What could we do that you hadn't already
tried at least once: drubbing me with your
tongue, smacking your lips in the kitchen.
What could we do that you hadn't already
done? I only wanted a sly kiss, red wine.

OUR BODIES

I

For years I've been meaning to expose you
to myself. Chewing a dried apple, I imagine

a surgical green room, your body petrified
but still breathing, steel cables restraining

your wrists like grisly tendons. I would sever
the arteries first, freeze them. In my easy

chair, I reread *The Bell Jar*, dropping crumbs
between the pages. Tea dribbles down my chin.

In a dream, my thumb is bleeding again, sliced
twice in the same spot while cutting weak tomatoes.

II

You said you could tell just by looking, with
my clothes on, I would be a tight fit. *It's all*

in the mouth, you said, *and the cut of your pants.*
Slipping into bed before curfew with no pajamas

on, like soaking lentils overnight: by
morning the beans are bloated, transformed,

ready for a quick stew, a wholesome meal, done
with the evening's sordid fluids. In another

dream I am upside down, walking on my hands,
ribs laid open like monkey bars for you to climb.

WINTER RITUAL

You have the lovers,
they are nameless, their histories only for each other,
and you have the room, the bed and the windows.
Pretend it is a ritual.

—Leonard Cohen, "You Have The Lovers"

You have the body's memory
of eggs purling calmly into
air. The last one rests,
resists release, nuzzles.
There is no shell;
a turbid film covers
the core. You've been warned
against this: seeds and germs
merging, spurning the others.
You have the lovers.

They are slow and firm and waiting
for the next snowfall. They've moved
closer into each other. They forget
the pull of the first cactus shoots in December,
coral filaments stretching toward the bed,
faint when turned over.
They forget the carton of skim milk on
the counter, the clotting of space
and membranes. Their lives hover.
They are nameless, their histories only for each other.

And you have the sun's spell,
the worsted throw, a tumbler of
tepid water on the nightstand. The pale dog
stirs with the radiator's pulse, pressing
itself into the frayed rug; the legs reach
in sleep for a murder of crows.
You have a clear vial, set on its
side, emptied of sandalwood oil.
The dog moans. A hollow door is closed.
You have the room, the bed and the windows.

Pretend you have fallen asleep in the room.
Pretend they are still in the bed. Pretend
you have the last poem, the last moment
inside the body's memory. The egg
settles. Skin makes skin. Seed recalls
seed. You have others to cull.
They are waiting for sublimation,
you have the bed, the cactus
burgeoning. The room inside you is full:
pretend it is a ritual.

CONFIDENCE TRICKS

I

After we drowned the centipede
in my sister's jacuzzi
we crawled into bed to remind
ourselves how we came to be together.

II

I was prepared like mustard.

III

The dog needs routine.
We're caught between the ropes.
Where were you when the warning bell went off?

IV

That summer was flat like Winnipeg
and I rode my bike through it,
though I might as well have been
a flightless parrot.

V

You told me the criminal mind lies
without concern for repercussion.
We are all lying.

VI

What did we learn in the end—that the end
never came?

If she were to start over, and she assumes this will happen sometime soon, she would move to Cape Breton. All she really wants is a small, clean house and several early nights in a row. She has always known that she could be anyone, any day, and she would like to think that she is moving forward, that she has somewhere else to be besides here. She would lie all afternoon, splayed on the creamy wool rug listening to film reviews on the radio, dreaming of Julie Ormond's cold persistence. She would let the phone ring, *69 every call, check the dial tone. If there were none, she might run to the back door, bolt it, lower the thick-slat blinds. She might hide in the pantry. She knows that everything would be fine if she had a TV, a VCR, if she had found an apartment with a bathtub instead of a shower stall, if she hadn't forgotten to pay for that bag of PEI potatoes the last time she was at the grocery store. Normally she would feel better by now. Her biggest fear is that one day she will give in and settle down like everyone else, move to a small clean house far from here and stay there.

She put the plaid flannel cover over the flattened duvet as soon as I gave it to her. Then she stripped to her black cotton underwear and crawled into bed. I went out to the kitchen to put the kettle on for tea, but was distracted by the drawing on the table. It was a drawing of my face, with a mustache and beard, and an extra mole at my brow. I went back into the bedroom to ask her about this, to find out what she meant to be saying, but she had already fallen asleep beneath the flannel's warmth. Now we are growing lint daily. We wake up with small blue tufts of cotton stuck to the hairs on our legs, in our belly buttons, between our toes. I watch the lint balls clump together in a sodden mass at my feet when I sweep them from my armpits in the shower. They swirl down the drain slowly, like lumps of soup catching in my throat—the kind of soup she calls gruel, especially if I put lentils or split peas in. Lately she has been leaving work early, arriving home with enough time to change and start dinner before I walk through the door. We have, simply, exchanged roles. I get up to do the dishes as soon as we've finished eating. I leave them to air-dry, draw a scalding hot bath with strawberry bubbles. Crouch in the tub like a frog, not letting my bum hit the foam, not letting my hands touch water. I balance like this until I can finally stand the heat, slide in up to my chin, watch the lint as it surfaces from my skin, and sinks.

V: THE MOMENT WHEN IT SEEMS MOST PLAIN

when you see the land naked, look again
(burn your maps, that is not what I mean),
I mean the moment when it seems most plain
is the moment when you must begin again

—Gwendolyn MacEwen, "The Discovery"

MILK

Push me or nudge me into drinking
the Earl Grey weak. You say, *It's the Irish
in you makes you like it milky*, and maybe
I'll sleep better this way, a sybaritic film
hovering like the memory of fingers
pressed into my belly. You would coat
your thigh with it if you could hold it
at all, if you could skim it from your idea
of me. I'm just a tiny rain fly, a moisture-
seeker, a speck stroked along the rim
of a fine-boned teacup. If I were sleeping
you'd find me, flick my legs lightly with
a thumbnail, grease the shortest path
for me downward while you swallow.

VINEGAR

Water or dry shiraz, and nothing else;
I'll pour a glass of each. You are a storm
leak through plaster, tuberculosis
before it is diagnosed. The first
time you drip like an intravenous
solution and I flinch at the needle prick.
Other nights you bead like mercury into
its own tarn and I can't watch you.
I will keep you in vials, save spittle
cells for gauging heat and health and
dips in pressure. The wine won't last.
There will be stains. The mole on my neck
will deepen, emerge as the black moth
you wait for. Soon my lungs will burn.

CRUST

Smear Bermuda honey across the pressed
sheet of pizza dough. Thick, sickly sweet.
This is what it's like to feed a single
girl these days: dry yeast, water, flour
a healthy flair for the dramatic
if company is coming, if it's been
too long. In another kitchen someone
she used to peel potatoes and scramble
eggs for makes a crust of his own, forcing
pastry into a warped foil pan while
the fetor of fresh minced meat rankles
his fingertips. Into the shell without
a spoon, a memory of red oleander
blooms and the blurred edges of his island.

CORE

Study her dry mouth: she's chewing popcorn
like a lady, lips sealed and prepared
for anything. In a week this might
startle, a sign of obdurate joy, but
you know she needs you now, her febrile
thighs reverberate mornings before tea
while you skim the smooth plane of her back
again. Wait for the throat's soft plangency.
Watch her take another bite, imagine
an unpopped kernel dropping like a loose
ball-bearing into the body's acidic dross.
Maybe her teeth let the pellet
slide, maybe her coming shakes free
a summer squall of caught morsels.

DILATE

Take the red chilies in my intestines:
I didn't chop them myself, didn't
need to protect a thumb or fingertip
from fire. I watched you do it all—toss
tofu in curry paste, turn crimped noodles
flaccid with boiling water—and where
could we go from there? You returned this time
as if parasites hadn't gotten
to you, as if your abdomen's
walls weren't wavering, straining to hold
it all together again. I told
you I couldn't sleep, sat in the armed
cherry wood chair like a kid with an old
jar, trying to catch fireflies for her collection.

WILT

In his dream I was hanged by a curtain
cord. He can't say why, only, *Women should
never drink wine. It pushes them over
the edge.* Does he remember the houseplant
we kept in the bedroom, on the ledge,
the blithe white cyclamen that bloomed
every month for a year? After this show
of strength and impudence, the bulb began
to rise, pushing through soil like a vexing
hernia, proffering blight. I moved it
from room to room, shelf to sill, hoping for
new-sprung moisture and what had already
been. When he left, the plant acquiesced,
flourished in the kitchen, kept the bulb high.

GIRL

She hands me her green sneakers, laces loosed
and ready for my summer feet to slip
inside the pliant canvas shell. Give me
yours, she says, as if this simple trade will
mark us, leave a spoor in every furrowed
space. We walk uphill to Silver Lake,
gravel dimples each of our thin soles
until we stop on the scorched shoulder
to rub the imprints from our toes.
She plucks two tomatoes from her small
knapsack, places one in my slick palm
and says, *I like to eat these like apples.*
I rub the firm blushed skin with my lips
and bite, tongue-tied, desiccated.

BOY

He licks the divot of my upper lip.
I sleep until noon, nesting. He says
the deuce is in him, in water,
in cries from the baby upstairs.
Lie with me. Lie with me again.
He shifts at dusk, supplicates and feeds
me secrets whisked into omelette froth.
He will waltz with two men on his
shoulders. He will skin me a peach.
And if he finds me wanting, sleeping? *Heal*
water, and from it there shall be no more
death or barrenness. The house is ready;
I slake the thirst for what I might lose
in order for this wakening to feel smooth.

LEAVING

Can't quite track the scent of his leg hairs through
winter wool pants from over here, but if
you could you'd trace his every egression.
Once, before his body hit that subfusc point
inside you, he asked if you ever hiked
alone. *Sure*, you told him, *late June
in grizzly country*, a day to yourself
while Cam pried arrant tourists from calving
elk. *Bell-ringing up the mountain path*,
as if you too had newborns to defend
against rented RV's and the perfidy
of strangers. *Wafts of dung and rank berries
trailed me*, you said, waiting for his furtive
pheromones to raddle your landscape.

HITCH

Anything can be fastened or bound
with the right substance. Travelling by train
to Jasper, we played Scrabble together
in the observation car, scanned northern
groves for moose, roved from coach to the bar
through those rubber-sealed steel doors, battling
bridling winds and variable velocities.
Back in our cramped seats, he changed, used
his penis like the bolt in a hasp
closure, a linchpin, hidden beneath
our Thinsulate sleeping bag. Every jerk
of that locomotive haunted me,
denied sleep, countered gravity. Getting
off, my legs buckled, aching to be still.

RED

You could wait all winter for the lure
of his mud-red shore, mussels ripped
from their craggy berths and soaking away
their sting in a plastic pail. You could
leave them there, stuck at the cottage door
in their own brackish rapture while you eat
raspberries one at a time, expecting
the silt to settle. But you don't.
Instead, pull a ruby turtleneck taut
across your milk-filled breasts, tuck
your hair behind your ears and dig in:
new tastes will kiss your tongue like roasted
pumpkin seeds, will multiply, will grind
the Fundy grit against your teeth, unrefined.

BLUE

Out of it, out of the blue, he finds me.
It's Sunday: we eat greasy prawns together
while my shins and thighs recall vascular
collapse. I want to pack the plastic air
between us with scraps of torn fabric,
a memory of thinned long johns and shredded
handkerchiefs. I might have drained that blue
blue blood from his smug lips, might have clipped
his fly-like wings and pinned them to my chest
like common scabs. I won't touch his arm now,
brushing past, the light thick behind painted
shutters. *It was as if you'd covered
me with a latex coat*, I'm telling him,
all colour and never enough contrast.

HAMMER

I was looking for a way into him,
a point like a piano key that could
be struck, or played, followed through with
a finger stroke or the full force heel
of my hand and still transmit its tonal
pulse to the intended string. He found his
way into me as if there were no felt
at all covering my small, embodied
hammers. Maybe, like a harpsichord,
my strings were simply plucked, with a quill
or some incised thorn of leather. Music
was never a direct hit with him: some
days the tune could resonate for hours,
others he lay mute, naked and controlled.

AXE

You can have your crazy squash, scattering
itself across the yard from the compost
heap. *Leave the milkweed and the loosestrife
alone,* you say, snatching my rusted shears,
snapping saffron touch-me-nots under
your boots. You hack at the teenaged
mountain ash, four more sharpened axes
hanging from your reinforced belt loops.
I want the blade to gasp within you, strip
strings from your slack, pernicious gut.
Inside, the house is like a garlic press
to you, squeezing your zest and bitterness
in a vice grip once I've nicked the bulb
and peeled the brittle layers from your skin.

DUST

Pale days keep you in bed with a lover's
hands offering the little deaths you hoped
for. Never by fanciful accident:
alone in a tin shed when lightning
hits the dull neck of the socket wrench
you were holding; locked below deck
in the hull of a docked ship, lungs
sucking at stale air until there is none.
No. The end you've memorized—by the cracks
around your father's eyes, apoplectic
veins and choked arteries—will be yours
to stop and start, to roll back behind
your lids with the body's gathered grit,
polishing the square root of your skin.

DECADENCE

My belly leaves a slight depression
in the broadloom when I get up from
the floor. It is difficult to lie. Ask
my thin-walled neighbours how often
they smell my burnt toast, hear my water's
cycled flush. Whoever built this off-white
house on a corner just needed some place
to live, didn't insulate the cheap dropped
ceilings, didn't ventilate the windowless
washroom. So I distend the fridge, harvest
gold, with incongruous delicacies: ripe
avocado pears, cashew butter. The rich
textures sate me, buffer my skin, deaden
the peal of pot lids clattering next door.

SNAILS

We can't snap out of this culinary
exchange for love: tonight he wrenches
snail bodies from their flawless encasements
and talks about baking them in pastry.
He hasn't done it yet, hasn't tried
to uncoil me, hasn't sniffed or probed
my sleep-filled temples for the mark
of a crow's talon, for the sinking of skin
and the unequivocal trappings
of weakness. There would be no foot to stand
on, my bones are scissor-sharp kitchen
tools, ready to separate meat from shell,
cake from springform pan. As if a sudden
slit in the right spot will leave us exiled.

HAWKS

Meticulous, young, he'd been hunting me
on the wing, losing speed in his descent
toward dinner. We met at the famed
tea room in town. I'd spent the evening
sticking out my tongue while winter trains
crossed the singing bridge. My naked teeth
were chilled. A single pot of tea was
steeping, warming the arborite table.
His fingers curved around my shoulders
like bark-sharpened talons before I saw
him, before I sensed the feral hook
of his hooded beak. I cleared my throat,
turned to gauge the breadth of his wingspan.
He wanted a new game. I looked away.

BREAD

He said it's always good to know which side
it's buttered on. I couldn't tell. And who
wanted access to those mundane details?
It was clear I'd had enough to eat by
then; I should have predicted the flight path,
the target, once I let the lone slice
fall—I made it, I broke it. Still, there can
never be enough bread and circuses.
In winter he liked it hot, overdone,
with a thick crust to knuckle-rap or rend.
I did it his way for a while, watched it
bloat and ferment, though I preferred to
mete it out before baking, shape it into
plaits or cloverleafs, to each their own.

WATER

Enough of milk. It sours in my mouth
like brine-swollen kalamata olives.
What stirs my tongue now: clear peppered
broth; the sun-struck freckles on your forehead;
zucchinis spoiling on the window ledge
before the rind wilts. I'll stay home
tonight, watch velvet strips peel from the quilt
on the east wall, scrub scallions for dip.
If you held me, pushed the soil away
from my aphid-like heart and held me like
the world's smallest bible in a walnut
shell, I would bend, would still be your shade.
Call it a stroke, a cycle of small shock
swells: the exact curve of the thing.

NOTES ON THE POEMS

The title "Preparations for Beautifying Women" is adapted from Esther 2:3.

The section titles in "Typologies" are from E. Annie Proulx's *The Shipping News* (1993).

"Self-Portrait as Ekphrastic Tension" alludes to W.J.T. Mitchell's discussion of ekphrasis in *Picture Theory* (1994).

Daisy and Violet Hilton (1908–1967) were conjoined twins who toured on the vaudeville circuit and were celebrated in such films as Tod Browning's *Freaks* (1932).

The first line of "Sackville, Season 2" is a reference to John Thompson's 'Ghazal x' in *Stilt Jack* (1978).

The final italicized section of "Boy" is adapted from 2 Kings 2:21.

The final line of "Water" is from John Thompson's 'Ghazal xxxvii' in *Stilt Jack* (1978).

ACKNOWLEDGEMENTS

Earlier versions of some of these poems were published in *Grain, Other Voices, The Fiddlehead, The Antigonish Review* and *Modomnoc*. Many thanks to the editors of each.

Thanks to Silas White, whose intuition and insights made the editorial process joyful; at UNB, thanks to Ross Leckie, Wendy Robbins, Holly Luhning and Melissa Walker, who each provided invaluable feedback on the manuscript; thanks to Carleton Wilson for his dedication to new writing; thanks to Sherry and Tom Finlay, Tracia Finlay and Tamara Finlay for their boundless support; and immense thanks to Drew Kennickell, whose love is unconditional and whose self-portraits in acrylic led me to a new place.